The Promise and Perils of Technology™

CYBERCRIME
AND YOU

Kristi Lew

Rosen YA
New York

For Bella and Maya, be safe. Love, always.

Published in 2020 by The Rosen Publishing Group, Inc.
29 East 21st Street, New York, NY 10010

First Edition

Library of Congress Cataloging-in-Publication Data

Names: Lew, Kristi, author.
Title: Cybercrime and you / Kristi Lew.
Description: First edition. | New York: Rosen Publishing, 2020. | Series: The promise and perils of technology | Audience: Grades 7 to 12. | Includes bibliographical references and index.
Identifiers: LCCN 2018043555| ISBN 9781508188223 (library bound) | ISBN 9781508188216 (pbk.)
Subjects: LCSH: Computer crimes—Prevention—Juvenile literature. | Internet and children—Juvenile literature.
Classification: LCC HV6773 .L49 2020 | DDC 005.8—dc23
LC record available at https://lccn.loc.gov/2018043555

Manufactured in the United States of America

CONTENTS

INTRODUCTION

Computers, smartphones, and other digital devices are used in homes, businesses, libraries, schools, and medical offices every day. According to the Pew Research Center, nearly 90 percent of Americans routinely use the internet to search for news and information, shop for goods and services, pay bills and conduct business, and communicate with friends and family.

The convenience of online shopping, remote access to banking, and the instantaneous streaming of entertainment has created opportunities for some people while posing challenges for others. One advantage technology provides is the freedom to access it from nearly anywhere, at any time. People no longer need to be in the same room, or even in the same country, to connect with a teacher, a student, a friend, or a business colleague. Television shows, movies, and stage productions can be viewed in any location at any time, rather than on a set schedule. Online stores are open twenty-four hours a day, allowing shoppers to purchase items around the clock instead of during limited business hours.

This freedom, however, may also come at a cost. Studies conducted by the American Psychological Association show that constant connectivity can be associated with higher levels of stress and anxiety in some people. Also, while the internet can allow people to develop friendships across the globe, it can also interfere with in-person, real-life relationships. In addition, criminals are increasingly

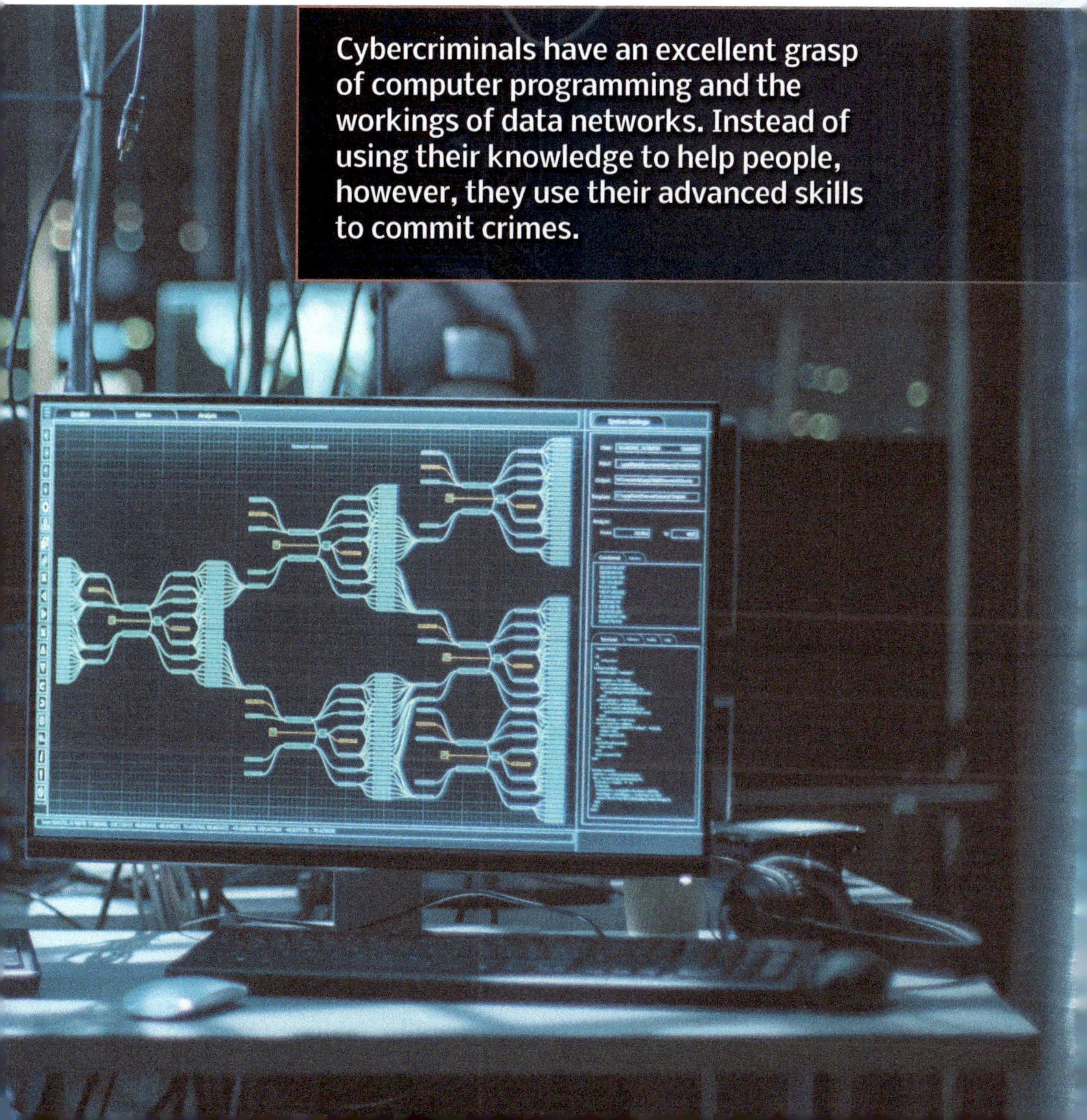

Cybercriminals have an excellent grasp of computer programming and the workings of data networks. Instead of using their knowledge to help people, however, they use their advanced skills to commit crimes.

using cyberspace as a gathering point, allowing them greater access to each other as well as to a growing number of potential victims.

Crimes committed using a computer or computer network are called cybercrimes. Some cybercrimes are simply new forms of older misdeeds. Fraud, theft, bullying, and stalking, for example, all existed before the invention of computers. Nonetheless, computers have made these crimes easier to perpetrate in some circumstances. Other types of cybercrimes are newer. Hacking and denial-of-service attacks, for example, are crimes that cannot be committed without the use of a computer.

Most of what ordinary citizens see online—online shopping sites, Facebook pages, YouTube, and the like—is part of what is called the surface web. These sites want and need to be found easily so that people can access and use them. There are other sites that do not want to be easily found. These sites do not appear in standard search engines, such as Google. The only way a person can visit these sites is if he or she happens to know the site's exact address. These sites are part of what is called the deep web or the hidden web. Then, there are sites that require special software, as well as special knowledge, to find them. These sites are part of the dark web. The dark web, or the digital underground, does have some legitimate uses. However, it also serves as a sanctuary or a hideout for cybercriminals.

Sometimes, it can seem as if a new cybercrime story is reported every day. A major retail store may announce that its system has been hacked and all its customers' credit card data has been stolen. A celebrity might reveal that private photographs have been leaked to the media. Government officials divulge their suspicion that foreign governments may have interfered with American elections. How many of these stories are true? Should private citizens be concerned? And, if so, how can they protect themselves?

CHAPTER 1

An Offer You Can't Refuse

Privacy and anonymity are essential to the people who use the dark web. These conditions may sound sinister, but criminals are not the only ones who feel the need to remain anonymous online. Journalists, in particular, may wish to speak with upstanding, concerned citizens who feel they might be in danger if their conversations or identities were to become widely known. Individuals living under an oppressive government may also use the dark web to access information on foreign websites without the fear of detection and possible government retaliation.

Hiding on the Internet

As necessary as anonymity may be for some people, the ability to become digitally invisible can also cause problems. In the shady corners of the dark web, criminals have set up an underground black market. There, they sell many products and services that cannot be sold in the open—from drugs and weapons to stolen Netflix logins and passwords. The dark web allows both the buyer and the seller to remain anonymous and, theoretically, untraceable.

Getting onto the dark web is not as simple as typing a website address into a standard internet browser. Instead, a free software tool called The Onion Router, or Tor, is required. Similar to an onion, Tor sends data through layers and layers of network nodes. Without Tor, a computer, mobile phone, or other internet-enabled device leaves behind unique identifiers called an internet protocol (IP)

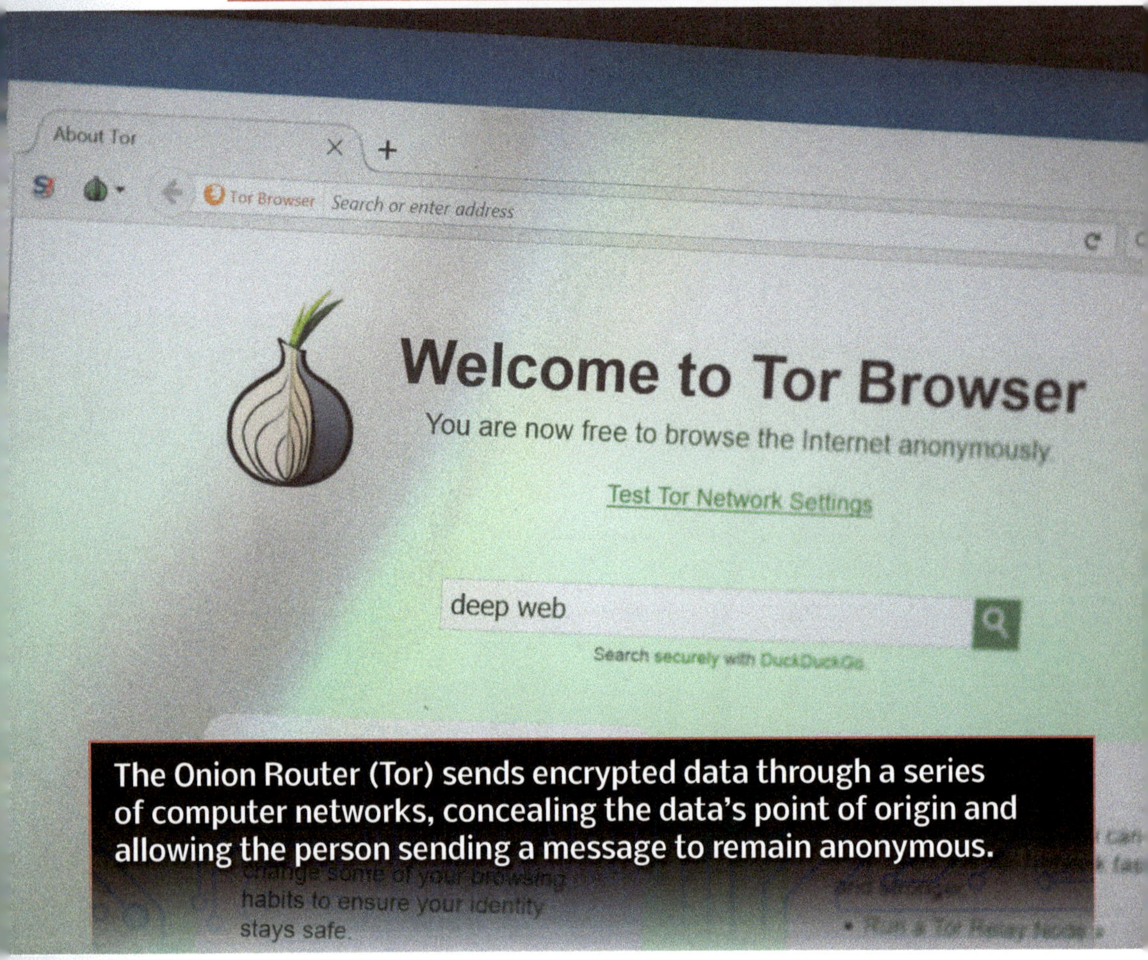

The Onion Router (Tor) sends encrypted data through a series of computer networks, concealing the data's point of origin and allowing the person sending a message to remain anonymous.

address and a media access control (MAC) address. These digital signatures can be used to identify the location of the network used to access the internet.

Tor, on the other hand, routes an internet connection through numerous worldwide servers, obscuring the true origin and destination. For example, if a cybercriminal in Cleveland, Ohio, wants to get onto the dark web, Tor might route his or her internet request through Cape Town, South Africa; Tokyo, Japan; Houston, Texas; Milan, Italy; London, England; and dozens of other locations before arriving at the true destination, which might be a website that lives on a network in San Francisco, California.

This rerouting of information and the cloaking of one's true identity can come in handy for a cybercriminal. Take, for example, a criminal set on committing cybertheft. Cybertheft takes place when a computer is used to steal someone's money, property, or information.

One way cyberthieves steal money is by setting up websites to sell counterfeit, or fake, goods. For example, a thief may sell fake tickets to a sporting event or a music concert. The unfortunate victims do not find out that their tickets are worthless until they try to get into the event and are denied entry. Other cyberthieves collect money for desirable goods—such as designer jewelry, watches, handbags, or clothing—but never deliver the goods. In these cases, the purchaser receives no product at all.

Why Pay When You Can Get It for Free?

Piracy is a different type of cybertheft. This crime involves the theft or the unlicensed use of copyrighted material. Copyright is one of the legal protections for intellectual property. Intellectual property includes items such as books, paintings, photographs or other images, computer software, inventions, designs, symbols, and logos.

Criminals sometimes try to make piracy seem victimless and, therefore, less harmful. Otherwise law-abiding citizens may accidentally turn into petty thieves when they are unaware of copyright law, too. Anytime someone uploads or downloads intellectual property protected by a copyright, that person is committing piracy, or copyright infringement. This situation includes actions such as downloading a video taken of a newly released movie in a theater, sharing a username and password with friends and family, using software paid for by an employer or a school on a home computer for personal use, or copying an online image and pasting it to a personal blog without permission. All these activities are illegal and fall under the label of piracy.

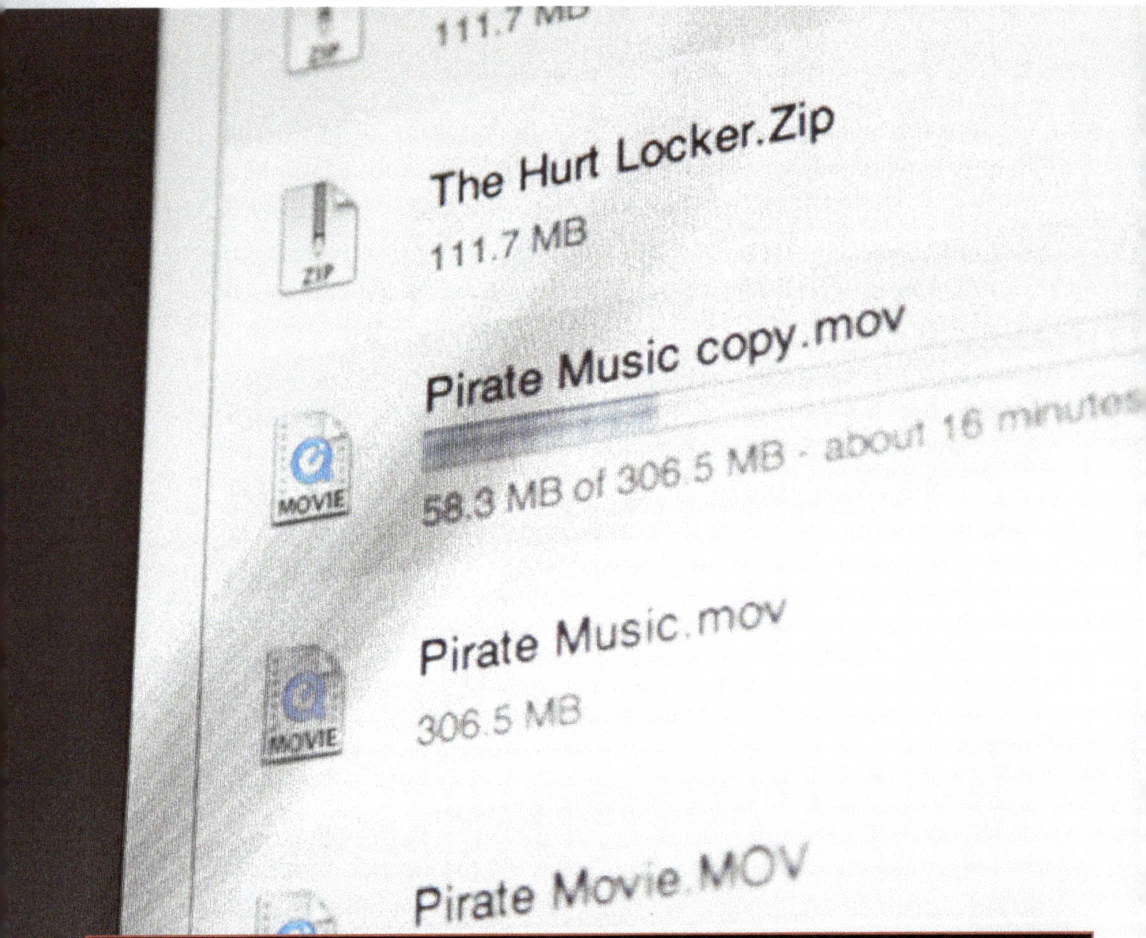

Downloading pirated music, movies, books, software, or other intellectual property may seem harmless, but it robs artists and other creators of their rightful payment for their work. For that reason, piracy is illegal.

Some people justify these actions by suggesting that the corporations these electronic items are stolen from do not need the money. However, these people do not take into account the fact that the authors, musicians, software designers, and other creators are also not getting paid. If enough people pirate their work, these artists cannot continue to create.

Baiting the Hook

Another type of cybertheft is phishing. Phishing is a type of social engineering. Social engineering is the use of human interaction to manipulate people into giving away private information they normally would not share. For example, a criminal might try to trick someone into revealing his or her username, password, bank account number, or other sensitive information.

Phishing is hacker spelling for fishing. People who spread phishing schemes by phone, email, instant messaging, tweets, or Facebook status updates are trying to get people to take the bait and give up their information. For example, a criminal might go online to find the social media accounts of employees in a specific business. From the social media accounts, the criminal can often find the employees' birthdays, spouses' names, children's names, where they went on their last vacation, and lots of other seemingly trivial information. The criminal can then call the company, claim to be from the company's computer division, and ask for a particular employee's username and password. While the criminal is waiting for the person on the other end of the phone to look up the employee's information, he or she makes what seems to be casual conversation where they drop little tidbits of information, like an employee's recent visit to France. The person at the company is tricked into trusting the criminal because he or she seems to know so much about the company's employees.

Phishing schemes can also appear to come from a legitimate business, such as the potential victim's bank, cable company, social media platforms, or mobile phone company. The email or instant message may threaten to close the victim's account if he or she does not respond. Or the message might say the user's account needs to be verified. The unsuspecting computer user, worried about the security of their bank account, credit card, or home loan, follows the directions in the message in the attempt to solve the problem. An

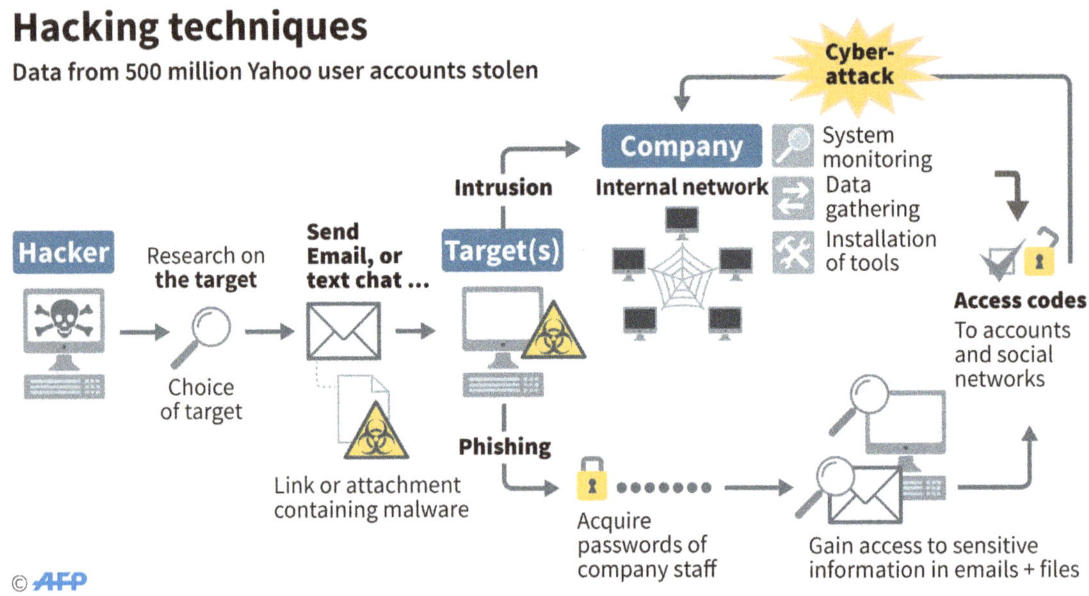

Hackers may steal passwords by finding a flaw in a computer system. They can also try to trick people into telling them sensitive information through phishing.

email or text message may direct the person to send their account numbers, passwords, or other sensitive information back to the sender. Alternately, the message may direct the person to click on a link that takes the person to a website that looks legitimate. Once on the site, the victim is instructed to enter his or her personal information. The victim does so because the website appears to be from a trusted company.

Another popular phishing technique is an email or text that says the person's credit card has been compromised. The message then instructs the victim to call a number. When the victim calls back, he or she is prompted to enter his or her credit card number. The beeps that correspond with different numbers on the phone's keypad are recorded and deciphered by the criminals. The credit card number can then be used online or printed on plastic to be used in a store.

Other phishing scams involve telling the victim that a friend or family member is in trouble while traveling abroad and needs his or her help. The email or text message appears to come from the friend or family member and pleads for the potential phishing victim to send money. The criminal gets the person's email address from his

Followers for Sale

Banking information and Social Security numbers are not the only personal information thieves are after—they also want people's social identities. Criminals steal names, pictures, hometowns, bios, education and job histories, likes and favorites, and other personal identifying information. They then use this information to impersonate the victim by setting up fake social media accounts. These accounts may be sold on the global black market. They are bought by people eager to have large numbers of followers so they can look influential on social media platforms.

These fake accounts may be used to promote pornography, violence, and other criminal activities. Sometimes, the criminals target the innocent victim's family and friends, sending them horrible messages that appear to come from their friend or loved one. These fake accounts can lead to unfortunate consequences, including damaged reputations and relationships. Unfortunately, social media platforms lag way behind cybercriminals in their security protocols.

or her friend's contact list. Never send money to "save a friend" until you have picked up the phone, dialed your friend's phone number, and actually spoken to the friend in person.

But It Wasn't Me!

Criminals may want usernames, passwords, bank account details, or Social Security numbers to steal money, but they may also be trying to steal someone's identity. This sensitive, personal information can be used to illegally obtain a passport, a bank loan, or credit cards under someone else's name.

Identity theft can have long-lasting effects. When credit card bills go unpaid, the victim's credit can be ruined. Damaged credit can result in higher interest rates, the inability to establish credit, and failed background checks. These consequences can prevent the victim from getting a job, buying a car or a home, or securing loans or credit cards in his or her name. According to the Huffington Post, people from the ages of eighteen to twenty-four, who are generally beginning to use their first credit cards, are one of the most-targeted groups for identity theft.

Young children are also a target for identify thieves. These victims are unlikely to have bank accounts or money to steal, but they do have pristine credit. In addition, it is likely they will not try to do anything with that credit until they are at least eighteen years old. They also do not get monthly credit card bills, where fraud might be easily caught. This lack of checks and balances allows the thief a long time to establish a credit file with no interference. In fact, the theft often goes undetected until the young person applies for a college loan and it is much too late. According to Javelin Strategy and Research, more than one million children had their identities stolen in 2017.

Once a criminal has enough information to pretend to be someone else online, he or she may commit crimes under that person's name, too. If the crime is detected, the identity theft victim

Children are prime targets for hackers. They can often be tricked into sharing personal information or clicking on a link that will install hacker-controlled software on the family computer.

may get blamed for it. In this way, innocent victims can be arrested for crimes they did not commit, end up with unjust criminal records, or saddled with outstanding arrest warrants. These issues can be very difficult to straighten out because the victim is unlikely to have evidence to show that he or she did not, in fact, do anything wrong. It may take years and thousands of dollars to clear the victim's name.

CHAPTER 2

Open the Door and Let Me In

Phishing is one way for criminals to access private information, but it is not the only way for them to get the data they want. People with a good grasp of how computers work can find ways around a computer system's safety protocols, too. Someone who specializes in breaking into computer systems is called a hacker.

Hacker Nation

Not all hackers have a criminal intent. In fact, at one time, the term *hacker* had a much more positive meaning than it does today. In the infancy of the internet and network computer systems, people who enjoyed programming computers would break into a computer system just to see if they could do it. These programmers, now called white hat hackers, simply enjoyed the challenge of besting the computer's security. Today, companies or governments often hire white hat hackers. The hackers' job is to look for gaps in computer security systems to learn how to improve them. White-hat hackers are security experts. They are called ethical hackers, red teams, or sneakers, too.

In contrast, a black-hat hacker is someone who breaks into a computer system to commit a crime or to cause harm. Black hats may deface or sabotage websites. They may intentionally change information to cause confusion or outrage. They can also steal personal information once they find entry into the computer system. They can then sell or use that information for criminal purposes.

Black-hat hackers break into computer systems to steal personal information that they can then use to commit a crime or to sell to the highest bidder.

Black-hat hackers are sometimes called crackers because their aim is to crack, or break, the system.

Gray hats are hackers who lie somewhere between white hats and black hats. Gray-hat hackers also search for weaknesses in a computer system. When they find one, they offer to give the

Hunting for Connections

Hacking tools are available for free on the internet. These tools are relatively easy to learn and use, even for people who are quite young. For example, during an ethical hacking event in 2015, seven-year-old Betsy Davies learned how to set up a fake Wi-Fi network in under eleven minutes by watching YouTube videos.

Curious kids aside, hackers intent on harm can easily set up fake Wi-Fi networks in coffee shops, libraries, or other public places. Once someone logs on to the hacker's network, everything that person transmits over that Wi-Fi connection is vulnerable to interception by the hacker.

Hackers can also get into home networks. Even networks that are password protected can be hacked. Many homeowners fail to change the default password that came with their router. There are entire websites dedicated to listing the default passwords for nearly every router in existence. Failure to choose a strong password can leave these homeowners vulnerable to being accused of a crime perpetrated through their home networks.

company recommendations on how to improve their security. However, they want to be paid to deliver the advice. Unlike white hats, gray hats do not start out as company employees. Nor do they have permission to break into the business's computer systems. Nonetheless, they are usually hacking to improve security rather than for a malicious purpose.

Another group of hackers are called hacktivists. Hacktivists are people who break into a website to promote a social or a political agenda. The word *hacktivist* is a blending of the words *hacker* and *activist*. Hacktivists are not usually after a financial gain. Instead, they may be trying to draw attention to their cause, raise donations, or persuade people to join their group.

Online companies use encryption software in an effort to prevent crimes. Encryption software scrambles customers' personal information so it is harder to use. However, many hackers are quite good at cracking this encryption as well.

Infected

Another way a hacker may gain access to a computer system is through a phishing scheme that persuades people to open an email attachment or to click on a link. The attachment or the website then downloads malware onto the victim's computer. *Malware* is short for "malicious software."

Once installed on a computer, malware can have various effects. Some types of malware damage the computer itself, leaving it disabled. Other types may delete files or steal information by acting as a remote keylogger. A keylogger collects everything that has been typed into the computer, including usernames, passwords, and account numbers. Malware can also allow the hacker to hijack, or remotely control, the computer system, including web cameras, which can allow the hacker to take pictures without the computer owner's consent. People are often unaware that malware has infected their computer. This ignorance puts them in danger. The longer malware goes undetected, the more information a hacker can gather.

The number of malware programs increase every day. Attacks on mobile devices are also growing in number. Viruses, worms, and Trojan horses are all different types of malware. Like their biological counterparts, computer viruses self-replicate, which means they can spread and infect other computers. Some viruses cause damage immediately. Others are programmed to lay dormant until a particular operation is carried out or a particular date arrives. The first widely known virus appeared on the Texas A&M University computer

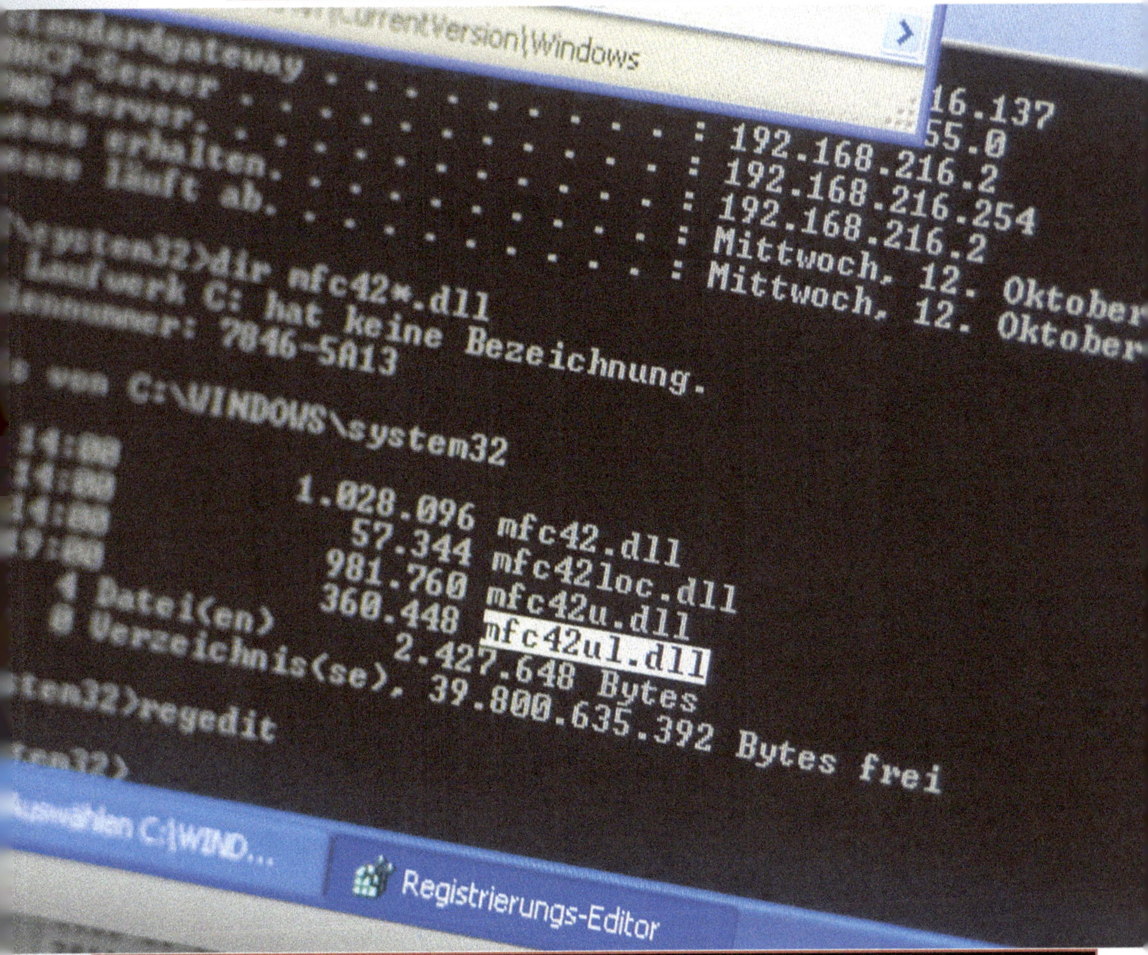

Malware is a file or a piece of software that is designed to damage or disable a computer network or to collect personal information without a computer user's knowledge.

system in 1981. The virus spread when students downloaded pirated computer games that were infected with the virus.

In May 2000, millions of computers running Windows were infected with the ILOVEYOU virus. This virus was also called the Love Letter virus or the Love Bug. The virus spread when people opened emails that had a hard-to-resist subject line. It said "I Love

You." Thinking they had received something nice, the computer user opened the email attachment and the virus immediately sent itself to the first fifty people on the victim's contact list. Once the virus was loaded, it erased music, photos, and other files. The ILOVEYOU virus eventually infected forty-five million computers around the world and caused an estimated $10 billion in damages. After an investigation, law enforcement determined that a man in the Philippines was responsible for writing and spreading the virus.

Like viruses, worms are malicious software. However, worms differ from viruses in that they do not require a computer user to open an attachment or to visit an infected website to activate the malicious code. Instead, worms are designed to find their way through network security holes. Once a worm infects a computer network, it can then spread to all the computers in the system.

Another type of malware is called a Trojan horse. This name is taken from a mythological story in which Greek soldiers invaded the city of Troy by hiding inside a wooden horse. Once the wooden horse was allowed inside the city walls, the soldiers poured out and the battle began. A computer Trojan horse is made to look like a legitimate piece of software or a requested file. When the file, like a Word document, for example, is opened, a piece of malware is installed on the computer.

A Hostage Situation

Another type of malware is called ransomware. Ransomware enables criminals to take over a computer system and shut it down. The hacker then extorts money from the computer owner. Only when the ransom is paid, will the hacker release the victim's computer and the data it holds.

Ransomware is often part of a spear phishing scheme. Spear phishing is a scam that specifically targets a particular person or website. Maybe, for example, the target owns a website where he or she sells products. The criminal crafts an email, gains the website

Bad Rabbit victims get a ransom note demanding payment before their computer files will be released. Depending on the exchange rate, 0.05 bitcoin can equate to between $200 and $400.

administrator's trust, and obtains the log-in information for the website. Once that step is complete, the criminal logs on to the website, changes the password, and locks the real website owner out. Then, the crook demands several thousand dollars in cash transferred to his or her account to restore the rightful owner's credentials. The criminal is holding the website hostage. Unless the person pays the ransom, that individual cannot regain control of the website.

Businesses struggle to stay one step ahead of the criminals. Criminal hackers and virus writers are very clever. They often outinnovate, outmaneuver, and outpace the antivirus industry. Business owners often pay ransom to regain control of their documents, photographs, and other files because it can be more expensive to get the ransomware removed than it is to pay the ransom asked for by the hackers. Patching security flaws may also slow down some computer networks, which costs the business time and, possibly, customers. However, technical advances are bringing security costs down and increased knowledge of security issues means more customers are demanding companies provide greater security for their information.

Request Denied

Another way hackers can cause chaos is by launching a denial-of-service (DoS) attack. A DoS attack can be activated after hackers get into a network and take over the computers, cell phones, and other internet-enabled devices on that system. Networks that have been taken over and are controlled by hackers are called bot networks or botnets. A botnet may be made up of thousands of computer networks, infected by malware that allows the hacker to remotely control all of them. Infected computers are sometimes called zombie computers, too.

Hackers can program botnets to request a specific website rapidly and repeatedly, sometimes at the rate of a million times a second. Servers that handle website requests can only respond to so many at one time. Botnets can quickly overwhelm the website servers, causing them not to respond to any requests, even legitimate ones. When the server stops responding, the website goes down. An inoperable website can cause significant economic damage to the targeted business.

In October 2016, for example, hackers launched a huge DoS attack that included PayPal, Spotify, *Wired*, GitHub, Twitter, Reddit,

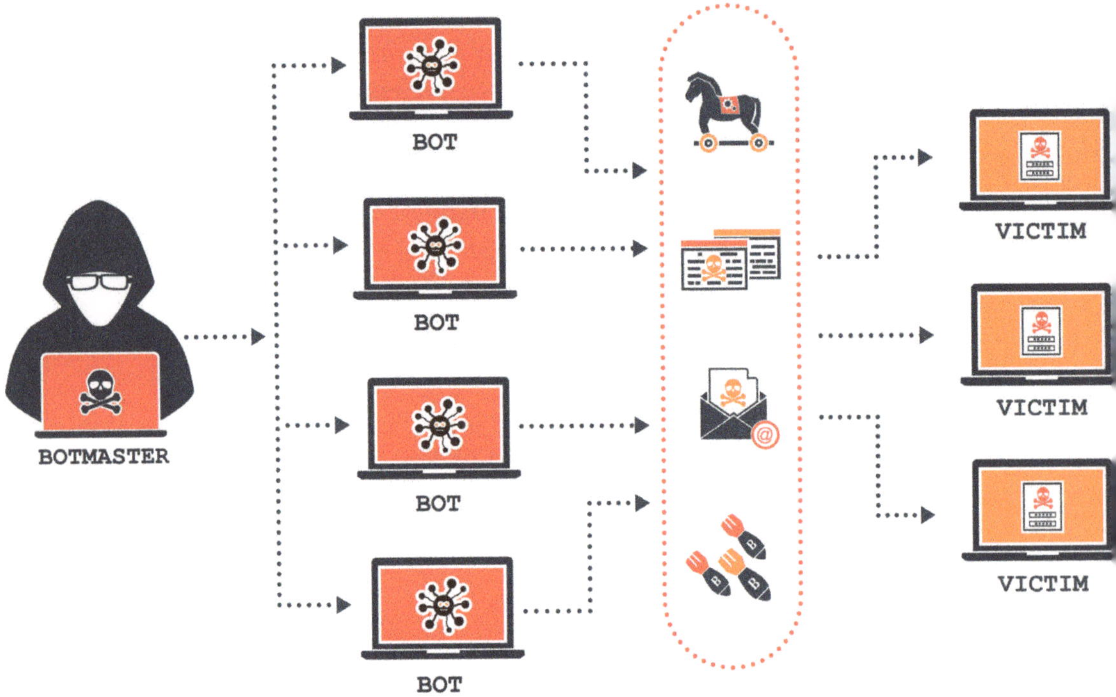

A hacker who controls a botnet is called a botmaster. The botmaster can instruct the computers in the botnet to distribute malware, perform a DoS attack, or carry out other illegal activities.

Netflix, Airbnb, and several other large companies. The masterminds behind the attack used not only computers and smartphones, but also other Bluetooth and internet-enabled devices, such as baby monitors, DVRs, security cameras, and thermostats. Security experts call these internet-connected, smart devices the internet of things (IoT).

US officials were originally concerned that a rival government had orchestrated the massive attack. They wondered if it was a practice run for disrupting the upcoming presidential election. However, when the culprits were eventually caught, it turned out that they had nothing to do with a hostile government. Instead, the authors of the malware that created the botnet were three college-aged men trying to excel at the computer game *Minecraft*. They never intended to take down the internet. Nevertheless, they were ultimately sentenced to five years of probation, 2,500 hours of community service, and ordered to pay $127,000 in damages for their part in creating, and then posting, the code to create an internet-of-things botnet. They could have gotten a much stiffer sentence and ended up in jail if they had not agreed to help the FBI and computer-security industry prevent similar attacks from then on.

Botnets are sold on the cyber black market for as low as $50. Hackers send the commands to the botnet through the internet, without the computer owner's knowledge. A computer system in the middle of carrying out a DoS attack may slow down, but this slowdown is often the only clue the computer owner gets that his or her computer is not really under his or her control. Security experts believe that as more smart devices become available, more people will be exposed to these security problems in the future.

CHAPTER 3

Let's Be Friends

The internet can be a great way to keep in touch with family and friends. It enables individuals to share events, photographs, and thoughts with people they rarely see in person. Social media platforms can also be wonderful tools for coordinating outings with people who live nearby and who share the same interests. Sharing information about their lives can certainly bring people closer together. However, it can also divide people into distinct groups and prevent them from meeting others with more diverse backgrounds.

You Big Bully

Although bullying has always been a problem in schools, the internet has brought bullying to an all-new level. Instead of having access to their victims only when school is in session, bullies can now harass their targets online at any time of day, year-round. Bullies can badger their victims through email, on social media, through texts, and in gaming apps.

A bully may masquerade as a potential friend or romantic partner, only to turn out to be a classmate, neighbor, or stranger who is intentionally trying to embarrass the victim. Many of the people targeted by online bullies have done nothing wrong. But this does not make being bullied feel any less terrible. Bullying victims still suffer tremendously, and it can seem as if there is no escape from the persistent harassment.

Internet bullies are sometimes called trolls. The term *troll* as pertains to internet bullies comes from a fishing method that involves

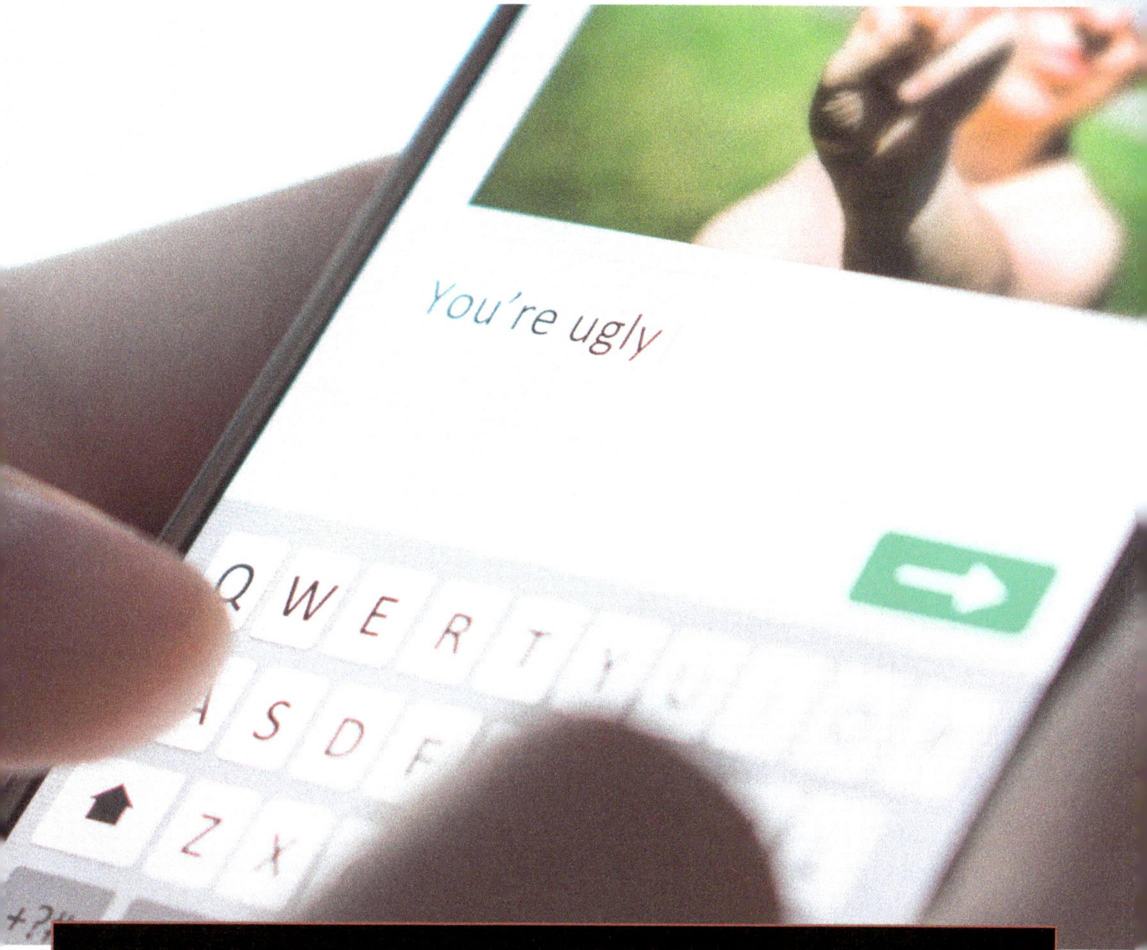

Cyberbullies use smartphones and other internet-connected devices to torment their victims. They may send hateful or threatening messages, spread lies, or take and post inappropriate pictures.

dragging a lure through the water as bait. Internet trolls bait by posting inflammatory, hostile, or provocative messages or images. Their aim is to evoke an emotional response in their victims, which makes the bully feel powerful. Trolls often pop up in comments on social media sites, news outlets, review sites, and in video game chats.

The best way to combat online bullying is to keep a record of interactions with the bully, but do not respond directly to his or her statements. Bullies are looking for attention. It is possible that they will move on if they do not get the response they want. However, do not ignore online bullying. When any instance of bullying is encountered, the best course of action is to report the person to school officials, law enforcement, or some other trusted adult. If an adult does not take the report seriously, persist until someone does. The ultimate objective is to get online bullies off the internet before they turn their attention to someone else.

Wherever You Go

Cyberbullying can sometimes escalate into cyberstalking. Cyberstalking is when an offender repeatedly tracks and shows up at the same online locations as the victim. The stalker intimidates the victim by flooding his or her email inbox, newsfeeds, or social networks with constant, unwanted messages, despite the victim's requests for the stalker to stop.

A cyberstalker may be a complete stranger or someone the victim already knows. Strangers may be attracted to a victim through his or her social media posts or pictures. They may create fake profiles to mirror the victim's interests to trick the victim into exchanging a series of messages. The stalker's objective is to gain the victim's trust. The behavior may then escalate to asking for an in-person meeting. Thinking she or he is meeting someone who has compatible interests, the victim accidentally put herself or himself in danger.

Social media also makes it easy to keep tabs on former romantic partners. Jilted boyfriends and girlfriends may keep up with former partners out of idle curiosity, but they may also become abusive. Online strangers may also be able to obtain detailed information about the victim through internet data brokers. These people specialize in finding physical addresses and phone numbers, often from the victim's social media posts or online databases. Stalkers

Cyberstalking can lead to permanent consequences. In January 2018, two twelve-year-olds were charged with and arrested for spreading online rumors about a classmate who, as a result, took her own life.

can use this information to leave notes, messages, or objects for their victims, vandalize their property, or to physically confront their victims.

When rebuffed, cyberstalkers may encourage others to harass or generally embarrass their victims. They may spread rumors about

Girls, Girls, Girls

In 2012, a Russian company launched a phone app called Girls Around Me. The app was approved and included in both the Apple app store and on Google Play. Taking advantage of location-enabled status updates and profile pictures on services like Facebook and Foursquare, the app would provide users with an interactive map of all the young women in their vicinity.

Once an app user found a profile picture he liked, he could go to the woman's profile pages to see what high school or college she had gone to, learn about her last vacation, find out the name of her parents, what her favorite drink is, what she has watched on Netflix, and many of the other seemingly innocent items people put online. Then, using this information he can casually walk up to the woman, wherever she is, and strike up a conversation. Because they seem to have so much in common, the woman may be more receptive to the stranger's advances than she would be otherwise, creating a potentially dangerous situation. The app is no longer available in either the Google or Apple app stores.

their victims or publicly humiliate them by setting up fake profiles that say embarrassing things.

Stranger Danger in Disguise

Many parents and teachers teach their children to be wary of people they do not know. Unfortunately, the anonymity of the internet allows users to pretend to be people they are not. A new online "friend," for example, may not be the person he or she claims to be.

Online predators make it their business to know the latest games, messaging services, and social networking sites that attract children and young adults. They will "groom" their victims by liking their posts, making flattering comments about their pictures, and claiming to be a boy or a girl of the same age. Grooming is a form of social engineering.

Cyberpredators often try to persuade the victim to keep their conversations private. The predator does not want a suspicious adult to know about the contact. The predator tries to sound like someone the victim's age and to convince the victim that he or she is romantically interested. The predator may then try to get the victim to send sexy pictures to the predator or to undress during an online video chat, which he records without the victim's consent. The predator can then use those images to blackmail and threaten the victim.

Amanda Todd, for example, was twelve years old when she was coerced into flashing her breasts on a live video chat. The anonymous person who made the request seemed nice and flattered Amanda about how pretty she was. Amanda assumed the requester was another teenager. However, a year later, Amanda received a message on Facebook from a man using a pseudonym, or a fake name. The man demanded that Amanda perform more explicit sexual acts on camera for him. He threatened to release the original video showing her topless if she refused.

Amanda decided not to give in to the blackmailer's demands. At that point, her tormentor set up a fake Facebook profile using Amanda's name. He used the photograph of her bare chest as the profile picture. Then, he began sending friend requests to all of Amanda's friends, teachers, and family members. Afterward, Amanda's peers blamed her for flashing her chest to begin with, and she was relentlessly bullied at school. Her parents tried moving to a new town, where Amanda went to a new school, but her online stalker followed and, once again, sent messages to teachers and students at

People around the world lit candles to pay tribute to Amanda Todd after cyberbullying resulted in the teen's death by suicide.

the new school. After years of constant harassment, Amanda could not stand it anymore. She committed suicide at the age of fifteen.

Years after Amanda's death, evidence led the Royal Canadian Mounted Police to the Netherlands. Police there identified thirty-five-year-old Aydin Coban as Amanda's persecutor. Dozens of other victims both in Canada and around the world were targeted by this pedophile. In 2017, he was sentenced to ten years and 243 days in prison for the online fraud, blackmail, and abuse of thirty-four young women and five men.

Young people are not the only ones fooled by online sexual predators. In 2011, police in Melbourne, Australia, uncovered a ring of child molesters who targeted single mothers with young daughters. The pedophiles searched online profiles to find single women who made references to or posted pictures of their children. Once they found a potential victim, the pedophiles used false names and social engineering techniques to start a relationship with the mother and worm their way into the women's homes. Eventually, the pedophile would successfully gain the trust of the mother and be left alone with his actual target, the woman's young child.

CHAPTER 4

Home of the Free

Individuals are not the only entities open to attack by cybercriminals. Governments, militaries, and businesses are vulnerable, too. Advances in technology have made many businesses and some parts of government more efficient. It has resulted in faster airplanes, laser-guided weapons, and unmanned bomb-carrying vehicles, which can keep soldiers safer. However, when government or military secrets fall into the wrong hands, many people may suffer.

The Shadow Brokers

The Shadow Brokers are a mysterious hacker group that surfaced in the summer of 2016. In August of that year, the group began to leak sensitive National Security Agency (NSA) secrets onto the internet. These secrets included the hacking tools used by the NSA to circumvent computer security. The NSA used these tools to get into the computers of adversarial groups and countries and spy on them.

The actions of the Shadow Brokers not only embarrassed the NSA, but they also handed cybercriminals a whole new toolbox of cyberweapons. Hackers worldwide have since used these leaked codes, developed at the expense of the American taxpayer, to create the WannaCry and Petya ransomware worms. These worms have been used against governments and businesses worldwide, causing billions of dollars in damages.

The NSA's failure to protect its own network has also deeply shaken the confidence of citizens and allies. The security breach

Governments may employ skilled computer programmers to remotely gather information about rival governments and radical groups. If the tools developed by white-hat hackers fall into criminal hands, the consequences can be dire.

has made many people question the agency's ability to develop and protect the sophisticated digital weapons that will likely be necessary in the future.

The Shadow Brokers are not the only group sharing hacking codes on the internet. In fact, there are numerous YouTube videos, online courses, websites, and books devoted to teaching people to

WikiLeaks and Whistleblowers

WikiLeaks is a website that was founded in 2006 by a hacker and activist named Julian Assange. Its stated purpose is to provide anonymity to whistleblowers who think information or data they have should be disclosed to the public.

Edward Snowden and Chelsea Manning are two names that often come up in discussions of whistleblowers and WikiLeaks. Snowden was a computer expert and former CIA employee, under contract with the US government when he copied and leaked millions of classified NSA documents. These documents showed that the agency was collecting the cell phone records of millions of American citizens. Snowden asserts that the documents prove that the NSA was spying on innocent citizens, which he believes to be illegal and unconstitutional. However, the documents also revealed programs that allowed law enforcement officials to monitor communications on the internet, including those among child sex trafficking offenders. Once these methods were uncovered, the criminals changed tactics, forcing international law enforcement to find new ways to decode their communications.

Chelsea Manning is a former Army intelligence analyst who leaked classified Iraq and Afghanistan war logs, videos, and diplomatic cables to WikiLeaks. Manning maintains that she leaked the information to expose military corruption and incompetence. However, her action may have also given adversaries an inside look at US military operations.

Whether people like Snowden and Manning are seen as freedom-loving, corruption-fighting individuals or traitors to their country is often a matter of opinion. However, whether or not they have broken laws is up to the courts. Manning was court-martialed in July 2013. She was released from prison in 2017. Snowden fled the United States. As of December 2018, he's living in Russia, having relocated there in 2013.

hack into computer systems. This being the case, hacking techniques can be learned easily and adopted by groups with minimal resources. This accessibility is wonderful if the hacker just has the public's best interest at heart, but it takes only a small group of computer-literate, radicalized zealots to cause massive, worldwide security problems.

Fake News

In February 2018, Robert Mueller, the special counsel investigating Russia's interference into the 2016 US presidential election, charged thirteen Russian nationals with illegally trying to disrupt the American political process. To achieve this disruption, the Russian agents are thought to have used fake social media accounts, political rallies, and online political advertisements to spread propaganda. Propaganda is information that is deliberately biased or misleading in nature. It is generally used to promote a particular political cause or point of view. The goal of this operation, according to many political analysts, appears to have been twofold—to undermine American citizens' trust in their electoral process and to polarize and deepen the division between the two major political parties.

The fake online accounts, also known as sock puppets, impersonated real Americans as well as creating fictitious ones. Some accounts focused on spreading divisive misinformation about issues such as immigration, the Black Lives Matter movement, religious freedom, and gun control. Other accounts specialized in spreading inflammatory messages to make it appear as if the opinions of fringe groups were more prevalent and powerful than they really are.

Many ordinary citizens believed the fake memes, cartoons, announcements, events, and news reports crafted by the internet trolls because they were shared by trusted friends, family, and news organizations. The result was a deeper division in the populace, a deep distrust in the election process and in each other, both of which may prove advantageous to foreign adversaries.

Sheryl Sandberg (*left*), a top Facebook executive, met with elected US officials after the company uncovered hundreds of fake accounts promoting misleading political messages during the 2016 presidential election.

Cyberwarfare

Cyberwarfare is the use of computer technology in a deliberate attack on a nation, business, or organization with the purpose of disrupting normal operations for strategic or military purposes. Many of the cyberattack tools that were once exclusively used by governments have become more easily obtainable, meaning these tactics can now be used by criminal gangs and, in theory, terror groups as well. Day by day, barriers to a terrorist cyberattack get lower.

Cyberspies are becoming more prevalent, too. Like spies of old, cyberspies seek intelligence on adversarial government agencies and competing political organizations. Unlike traditional acts of espionage, however, cyberspies obtain this information by infiltrating websites and rooting out classified information.

Readily available spyware allows remote activation of microphones, cameras, and location services on smartphones, allowing the person who installed the app to listen in on a conversation or access the phone's Global Positioning System (GPS). Access to the GPS can not only track the location of the phone (and the person carrying it), but it can also send a text when the target leaves a designated area, allowing that person to be followed.

In 2011, the US military changed its policy on cyberattacks. The military today views any online attack as an act of aggression, meaning that a cyberattack may be met by an offline, physical showing of military might. Cyberattacks include espionage (spying), sabotage (including denial-of-service attacks and attempts to disrupt the electrical power grid), and the spread of propaganda.

Ukraine and Russia have been locked in a cyberwar since at least 2015 when a team of Russian hackers, known as Sandworm, hacked into dozens of Ukrainian governmental organizations and companies. The group was able to penetrate the computer security of networks from media outlets to transportation firms. Once inside, they detonated logic bombs that destroyed terabytes of data, costing companies billions of dollars in lost data and sales. Their attacks also affected ordinary Ukrainian citizens when, during that brutally cold winter, the saboteurs caused widespread power outages.

In spring 2017, Russian military hackers hijacked the network of a small, family-run Ukrainian software company. The company's network of computer servers are used to send out routine updates—such as bug fixes, security patches, and new features—to a piece of accounting software used by nearly everyone who files taxes or does business in Ukraine. The military hackers installed an update

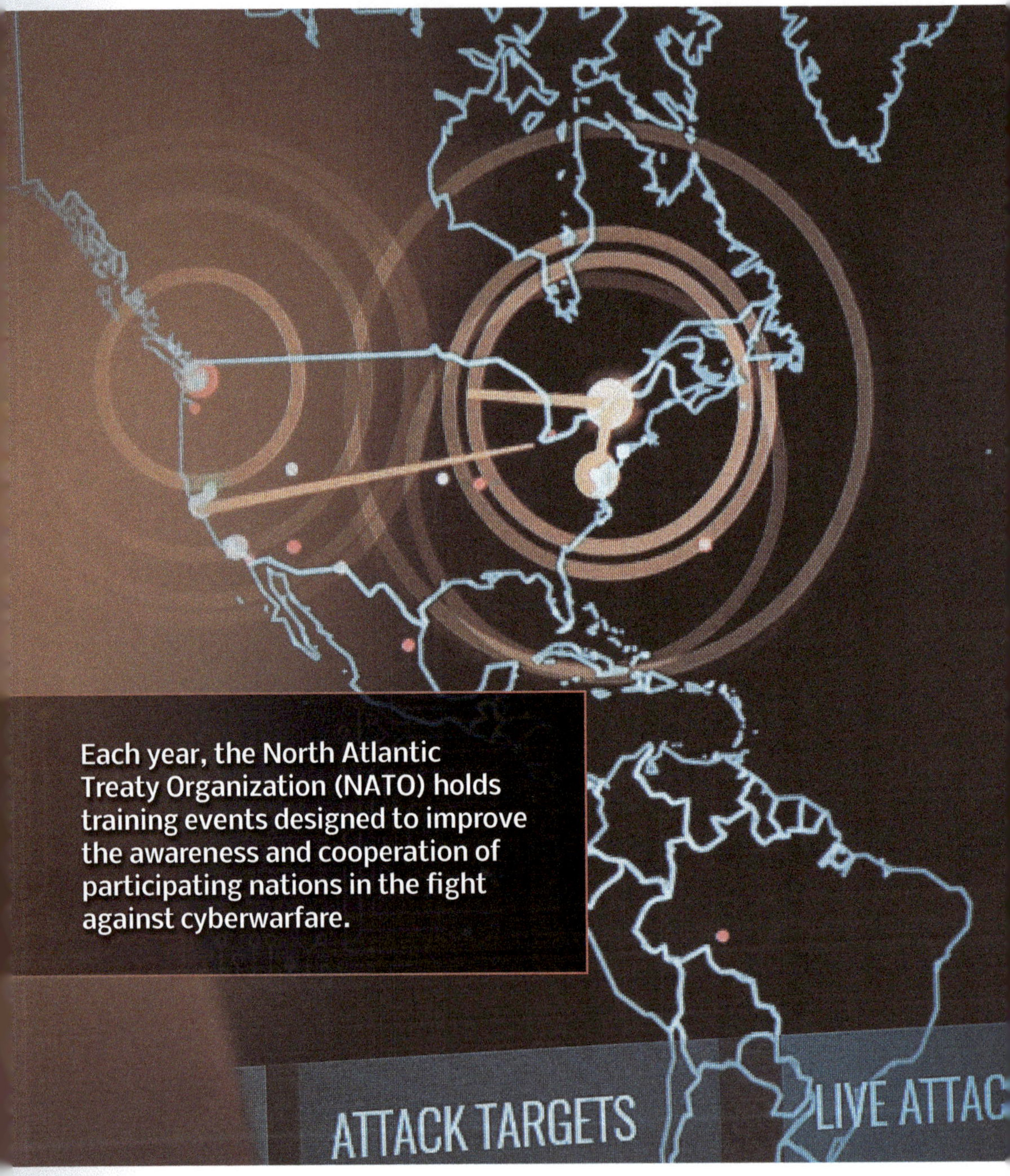

Each year, the North Atlantic Treaty Organization (NATO) holds training events designed to improve the awareness and cooperation of participating nations in the fight against cyberwarfare.

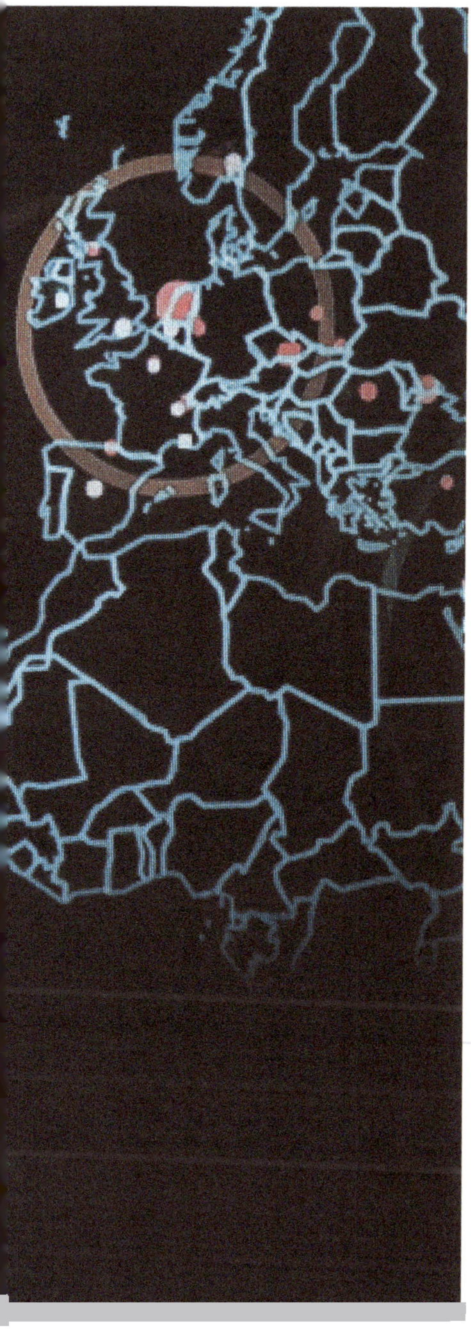

that created a hidden back door into any computer that had the accounting software installed. Then, in June 2017, hackers used that back door to release a piece of malware called NotPetya.

NotPetya was programmed to irreversibly encrypt the computer's master boot record. This program tells the computer where to find its operating system. Without it, the computer will not start and all its data is lost. The worm was also programmed to automatically and rapidly infect any computer that came into contact with it. It took NotPetya forty-five seconds to bring down the entire network of a large Ukrainian bank. In all, NotPetya brought down the computers in at least four hospitals in Kiev, the capital city, six power companies, two airports, nearly every federal agency, and more than twenty-two Ukrainian banks, including ATMs and credit card payment systems. The Ukrainian government shut down, and more than three hundred companies had their computer networks destroyed. In addition, with the credit card payment system down, citizens across the country started to panic.

In the summer of 2017, malware effectively shut down banking operations in Ukraine, causing the public to worry about how long their money would remain inaccessible.

Would they have enough cash for groceries and gas to outlast the cyber invasion?

Within hours of its release, the program raced through Ukraine and into cyberspace beyond the country's borders. Ultimately, NotPetya would spread around the world—from hospitals in Pennsylvania to multinational companies, including the pharmaceutical giant Merck and a European subsidiary of FedEx. It even spread back to Russia and infected the state oil company. According to an article in *Wired*, written by Andy Greenberg, the release of this piece of malware has caused more than $10 billion in total damages as of August 2018.

One thing NotPetya clearly illustrated was how vulnerable the infrastructure of the modern world is to cyberattack. No longer does an adversarial country's military have to set foot on foreign soil to engage in battle. Distance is no longer a good defense. Weapons of war can now be released in a medium where no national boundaries exist. Global corporations are interconnected, not only within their far-flung offices but also to one another. The global networks that have unified and elevated businesses of the world over the past twenty-five years could come crashing down over the span of a few hours. Without computer connections, supermarkets would shut down, people could not get money out of a bank or ATM, airplanes would cease to fly, and power companies would be unable to distribute power.

CHAPTER 5

Safe Surfing

In the last few decades, technology has made crime fighting much easier than it had been previously. Law enforcement officials use the internet and social media for leads and sources for information. Nevertheless, all online systems have vulnerabilities. People must assume that any online platform can and will be hacked. When that occurs, personal information can be laid bare. The key to remaining safe online is to know where digital threats exist and how to take appropriate precautions to secure sensitive data.

Staying Safe Online

Most computer systems have some kind of security to prevent hackers from entering and stealing information. A firewall is part of that security system. Firewalls are designed to allow outgoing communication but to restrict incoming requests for access. Experienced hackers, skilled at programming, can often get through a firewall. Still, it is worthwhile to keep information behind a firewall to prevent casual hacking attacks.

Using strong passwords is another way to keep information safe. Strong passwords consist of more than six characters, which should be a combination of capital and lowercase letters, numbers, and symbols. It is best to use different passwords for every site on the internet. However, some people find it difficult to remember so many passwords. A password vault program can help with this problem. These programs encrypt all a computer user's passwords and keep

Strong passwords can be hard to remember unless there is an underlying system used as a mnemonic device. Automated password management programs can help avoid this issue.

them in a secure area of the computer. Another way to remember different passwords for different websites is to invent a particular pattern—for example, the first four letters of the website name, a series of numbers that correspond to the positions of those letters in the alphabet, followed by the first letters of a specific phrase—and use that pattern with every website.

Never share log-in or password information. First, doing so with the intention of allowing others access to copyrighted digital media, such as books, movies, games, and software, is illegal. Also, emails that ask for such sensitive information are almost always scams. Do not click on a link or download an attachment sent through email. Instead, type the website address directly into the internet browser. If a bank, credit card company, or cell phone service really needs the information the email is seeking, a message should appear once the customer has logged in to the site.

Set all social media privacy settings as high as they will go and password protect your home Wi-Fi network. If two-factor authentication (TFA) is available, use it. TFA is an additional layer of security in which your account can be accessed only by trusted devices. To sign on from a different device, a code is sent to your phone, tablet, or another trusted computer.

No matter who asks for it, never send a photo or a video that you would not want made public. If you are being bullied or stalked online or if anyone asks for anything inappropriate, discuss your concerns with a trusted adult as soon as possible.

Catching Cybercriminals

Many countries, including the United States, have laws that make cybercrime illegal. Often, however, the laws lag behind technology, which results in laws that are outdated before they are passed.

According to the National Conference of State Legislatures (NCSL), all fifty US states have laws to address cybercrime. Most of these laws focus on unauthorized access and trespassing (that is, hacking) as well as the creation and distribution of malware. Twenty-five states have laws making it illegal to launch a denial-of-service attack. Five states specifically target computer extortion in their legislation, while other states include ransomware in their statutes that outlaw malware. In 2018, the Cyber Civil Rights Initiative reported that forty states and the District of Columbia have laws against

Digital Forensics

Digital forensics is the branch of forensic science that includes the identification, preservation, recovery, and investigation of evidence found on a suspected criminal's computer, cell phone, and other electronic devices. Before they can analyze data on someone's computer, cybersecurity experts must first find the data.

Data can be stored on a computer's hard drive, of course, but it may also reside on external hard drives, flash drives, and network servers. Once the data is found, a computer forensic scientist must copy the data without compromising the original. The reason that he or she makes a copy is so that the original data is preserved during the investigation. If the data is changed, damaged, or lost, the evidence cannot be used in court.

Once the data is copied, the forensic expert gets to work recovering and analyzing potential evidence. This information may include deleted files. Even though a deleted file seems to disappear, data belonging to that file stays on the computer's hard drive until it is overwritten. Specialized file-recovery software can often retrieve parts of a file, or even the entire file, which can then be pieced together to provide evidence of a crime.

nonconsensual pornography, which involves posting photographs or videos of someone in a sexually compromising position without the person's permission. Possessing or asking for pictures of a minor (someone under the age of eighteen) that are sexual in nature is a federal offense.

Technology can be a double-edged sword. Sometimes, law enforcement officials can use technology to catch crooks, but the size, speed, and anonymity of the internet also makes it easy for criminals to evade detection and capture.

A digital forensics expert looks for trace evidence on a computer memory chip using a 3D microscope. Trace evidence includes carpet or clothing fibers and hair or other biological samples.

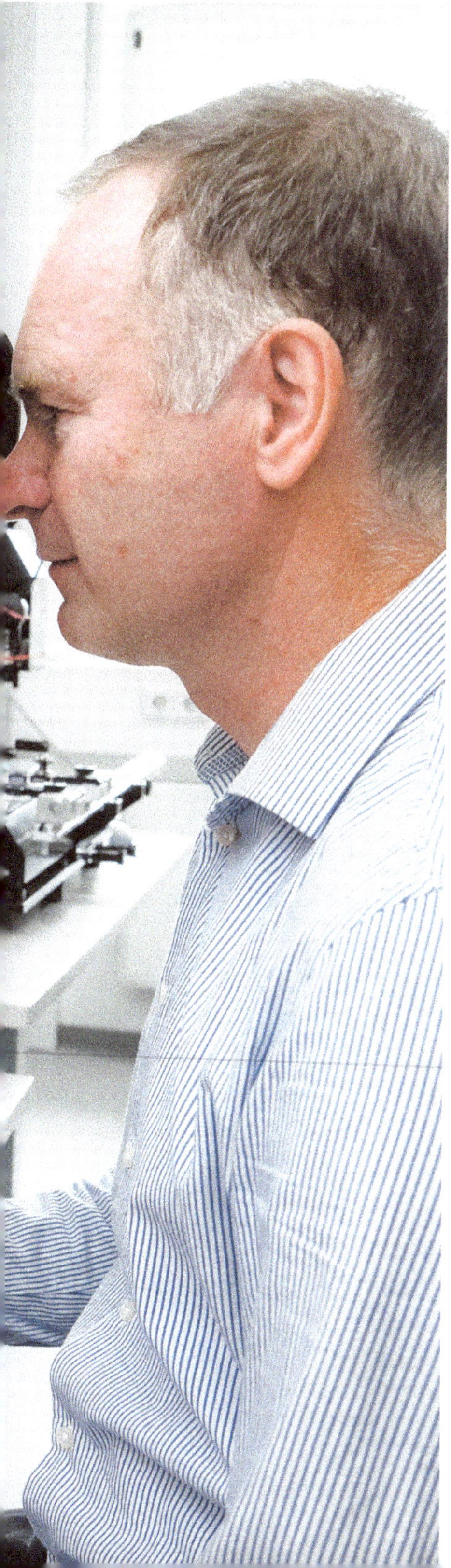

Cybercriminals do not always commit crimes where they live. In fact, they may live thousands of miles away, on a completely different continent, from their victims. In addition, a specific cybercrime may be considered illegal in one country but not in another. Various cultures view the freedoms afforded to an individual differently, too, and not all countries have robust computer security forces. All these issues mean that even when law enforcement agencies in different countries work together, cybercriminals often get away with their crimes.

Sometimes law enforcement is not even aware that a crime has been committed. Many cybercrimes go unreported. People may be embarrassed if they have fallen for phishing schemes, and they do not want to call the police and reveal the depth of their gullibility. Other people are unaware that their information has been stolen. Businesses may not report hacking incidences because company executives are afraid of

An IBM executive speaks to global leaders at an international cybersecurity conference. Computer experts all over the world must work together to curb cybercrime and ensure the safety of worldwide computer networks.

losing their customers' confidence in the company's ability to keep sensitive information safe.

Above all, digital citizenship requires all computer users to think critically about any request to divulge personal information. Examining news or messages posted online for underlying bias and implied messages is important, too. Critical thinking can help combat propaganda, fight social engineering, and help people avoid getting snared by hackers or online predators. As the world becomes ever more dependent on technology, the quality of future interactions within the digital environment will depend on the ability of the smart, capable people who inhabit cyberspace to keep themselves and others safe from harm.

Glossary

anonymity The state of being unknown or nameless.

cyberspace The system of computer networks that store, share, and communicate information online.

denial-of-service (DoS) attack A cybercrime designed to overwhelm a website server with numerous requests in an attempt to render the website useless.

espionage Spying, especially by governments to get certain information.

firewall A part of a computer's security system that allows outgoing communication but that restricts access to incoming requests.

hacker A computer programming expert with the ability to subvert computer security protocols.

internet of things (IoT) Everyday objects that send and receive data via the internet.

logic bomb Code embedded in malware that is designed to execute certain instructions, often destructive, when a particular condition is met.

malware Software intended to cause harm or to destroy computer networks.

network A group of linked computer hardware devices.

perpetrate To carry out a crime or other hurtful act.

phishing The act of sending fraudulent emails with the intention of tricking someone into revealing sensitive, personal information.

piracy The illegal uploading, downloading, or sharing of copyrighted digital material.

propaganda Intentionally misleading information designed to promote a particular political position or point of view.

provocative Causing anger or excitement on purpose.

router A piece of hardware that forwards packets of data from one computer to another, thereby directing traffic on the internet.

security protocols The rules and operations that protect data and computer networks from hackers and cybercriminals.

social engineering A set of techniques designed to gain someone's trust to manipulate that person into breaking normal computer safety protocols.

sock puppet A false online identity created to spread a particular political point of view or opinion.

Trojan horse A piece of code that masquerades as a legitimate software program or file but, once downloaded, installs a piece of malware on the infected computer.

two-factor authentication An extra layer of security that requires not only a username and password but also a code sent to a separate trusted device.

virus A type of malware that relies on human actions to help it spread from computer to computer.

whistleblower An employee or other insider who informs the public of illegal or questionable actions within a company or government.

worm A type of malware that does not require human action to spread through a computer network.

Canadian Advanced Technology Alliance

207 Bank Street, Suite 416
Ottawa ON K2P 2N2
Canada
(613) 236-6550
Website: https://cata.ca
Email: info@cata.ca
Facebook and Twitter: @CATAAlliance
The Canadian Advanced Technology Alliance is an advocacy group devoted to keeping digital technologies safe. The group hosts a cybercrime summit that brings together police, industry and government officials, and academic leaders to exchange information on current cybercrime trends as well as maintaining a website that provides a collection of articles on cybersecurity and best practices.

Center for Internet Security (CIS)

31 Tech Valley Drive
East Greenbush, NY 12061
(518) 266-3460
Website: https://www.cisecurity.org
Facebook: @CenterforIntSec
Twitter: @CISecurity
The Center for Internet Security provides the latest in cybersecurity best practices, tools, and threats. The organization also hosts the US Cyber Challenge (https://www.uscyberchallenge.org), which strives to identify and recruit the next generation of cyber talent through ethical hacking summer camps and online quests.

Cyber Civil Rights Initiative

University of Miami School of Law
1311 Miller Road, G-378
Coral Gables, FL 33146
(844) 878-2274
Website: https://www.cybercivilrights.org
Email: info@cybercivilrights.org
Facebook: @CyberCivilRightsInitiative
Twitter: @CCRInitiative
The Cyber Civil Rights Initiative is an advocacy group that provides support and fights for justice for victims of cybercrime.

Electronic Frontier Foundation

815 Eddy Street
San Francisco, CA 94109
(415) 436-9333
Website: https://www.eff.org
Email: info@eff.org
Facebook and Twitter: @EFF
The Electronic Frontier Foundation is a nonprofit organization that defends free speech online, fights illegal surveillance of innocent citizens, and advocates for digital rights and freedoms.

Federal Bureau of Investigation (FBI)

935 Pennsylvania Avenue NW
Washington, DC 20535-0001
(202) 324-3000
Website: https://www.fbi.gov

Email: WFOCOP@fbi.gov
Facebook and Twitter: @FBI
The FBI website includes the latest cybercrime news, the cybercrime most-wanted list, and a safe online surfing program to educate children in grades three to eight on the importance of cybersafety.

Identity Theft Resource Center

3625 Ruffin Road, #204
San Diego, CA 92123
(888) 400-5530
Website: https://www.idtheftcenter.org
Email: itrc@idtheftcenter.org
Facebook and Twitter: @ITRCSD
Instagram: @idtheftcenter
The Identity Theft Resource Center provides victims of identity theft with the resources they need at no cost to help clear their names as quickly as possible. The group also provides identify theft prevention education and training.

National Crime Prevention Council

2614 Chapel Lake Drive, Suite B
Gambrills, MD 21054
(443) 292-4565
Website: https://www.ncpc.org
Facebook: @McGruff
Twitter: @McGruffatNCPC
The National Crime Prevention Council provides programs to inform parents and children on how to spot and stop

cyberbullying, intellectual property theft, and fake consumer goods. It offers programs to educate the public on how to use the internet securely.

Office of the Privacy Commissioner of Canada

30 Victoria Street
Gatineau, QC K1A 1H3
Canada
(800) 282-1376
Website: https://www.priv.gc.ca/en
Facebook: @PrivCanada
Twitter: @PrivacyPrivee
The Office of the Privacy Commissioner of Canada oversees how businesses and government institutions collect, handle, and use Canadian citizens' private information. Their website provides information on individual privacy rights, privacy laws, and tips on how to protect personal information.

For Further Reading

Anniss, Matt. *Cyber Wars*. New York, NY: Cavendish Square, 2018.

Bodden, Valerie. *Digital Forensics*. Mankato, MN: Creative Education Creative Paperbacks, 2018.

Di Piazza, Domenica. *Google Cybersecurity Expert Parisa Tabriz*. Minneapolis, MN: Lerner Publications, 2018.

Furgang, Kathy. *Internet Surveillance and How to Protect Your Privacy*. New York, NY: Rosen Publishing, 2017.

Hand, Carol. *Using Computer Science in High-Tech Criminal Justice Careers*. New York, NY: Rosen Publishing, 2018.

Hubbard, Ben C., and Diego Vaisberg. *My Digital Rights and Rules*. Minneapolis, MN: Lerner Publications, 2018.

Hurt, Avery Elizabeth. *Everything You Need to Know About Sextortion*. New York, NY: Rosen Publishing, 2018.

Kamar, Haq. *What Is Cybersecurity?* New York, NY: Britannica Educational Publishing, 2018.

Kamberg, Mary-Lane. *Cybersecurity: Protecting Your Identity and Data*. New York, NY: Rosen Publishing, 2018.

Karpan, Andrew. *Troll Factories: Russia's Web Brigades*. New York, NY: Greenhaven Publishing, 2018.

Loh-Hagan, Virginia. *Ethical Hacker*. Ann Arbor, MI: Cherry Lake Publishing, 2016.

Lüsted, Marcia Amidon. *Hacking and Freedom of Information*. New York, NY: Greenhaven Publishing, 2018.

Machajewski, Sarah. *Identity Theft in the 21st Century*. New York, NY: Lucent Press, 2018.

McAneney, Caitie. *I Have Been Cyberbullied, Now What?* New York, NY: Rosen Publishing, 2016.

Porterfield, Jason. *White and Black Hat Hackers*. New York, NY: Rosen Publishing, 2017.

Sciandra, Mike. *Cybercrime: Using Computers as Weapons*. New York, NY: Lucent Press, 2018.

Senker, Cath. *Cybercrime and the Darknet: Revealing the Hidden Underworld of the Internet*. London, UK: Sirius, 2017.

Steffens, Bradley. *Securing Cyberspace*. San Diego, CA: ReferencePoint Press, 2018.

Timmons, Angie, and Sara L. Latta. *Investigating Cybercrime*. New York, NY: Enslow Publishing, 2018.

Wiener, Gary. *Cyberterrorism and Ransomware Attacks*. New York, NY: Greenhaven Publishing, 2018.

Wilkinson, Colin. *Everything You Need to Know About Digital Privacy*. New York, NY: Rosen Publishing, 2018.

Yearling, Tricia. *How Do I Stay Safe from Cyberbullies?* New York, NY: Enslow Publishing, 2016.

Bibliography

CBC News. "Man Accused of Extortion of Amanda Todd Sentenced to Jail in Netherlands." Canadian Broadcasting Corporation, March 15, 2017. https://www.cbc.ca/news/canada/british-columbia/man-accused-of-extortion-of-amanda-todd-sentenced-to-jail-in-netherlands-1.4027293.

Cimpanu, Catalin. "Mirai Botnet Authors Avoid Prison After 'Substantial Assistance' to the FBI." September 19, 2018. https://www.zdnet.com/article/mirai-botnet-authors-avoid-prison-after-substantial-assistance-to-the-fbi.

Cyber Civil Rights Initiative. "40 States + DC Have Revenge Porn Laws." Retrieved October 19, 2018. https://www.cybercivilrights.org/revenge-porn-laws.

Faris, Rob, Hal Roberts, Bruce Etling, Nikki Bourassa, Ethan Zuckerman, and Yochai Benkler. "Partisanship, Propaganda, and Disinformation: Online Media and the 2016 U.S. Presidential Election." Harvard University, August 16, 2017. http://cyber.harvard.edu/publications/2017/08/mediacloud.

Goodman, Marc. *Future Crimes*. New York, NY: Doubleday, 2015.

Graff, Garrett. "How a Dorm Room Minecraft Scam Brought Down the Internet." *Wired*. December 13, 2017. https://www.wired.com/story/mirai-botnet-minecraft-scam-brought-down-the-internet.

Greenberg, Andy. "The Untold Story of NotPetya, the Most Devastating Cyberattack in History." *Wired*, August 22, 2018. https://www.wired.com/story/notpetya-cyberattack-ukraine-russia-code-crashed-the-world.

Hill, Joshua B., and Nancy E. Marion. *Introduction to Cybercrime: Computer Crimes, Laws, and Policing in the 21st Century.* Santa Barbara, CA: Praeger, 2016.

National Conference of State Legislatures. "Computer Crime Statutes." June 14, 2018. http://www.ncsl.org.

Parlapiano, Alicia, and Jasmine C. Lee. "The Propaganda Tools Used by Russians to Influence the 2016 Election." *New York Times*, February 16, 2018. https://www.nytimes.com/interactive/2018/02/16/us/politics/russia-propaganda-election-2016.html.

Pascual, Al, and Kyle Marchini. "2018 Child Identity Fraud Study." Javelin Strategy & Research, April 24, 2018. https://www.javelinstrategy.com/coverage-area/2018-child-identity-fraud-study.

Schneier, Bruce. "Who Are the Shadow Brokers?" *Atlantic*, May 23, 2017. https://www.theatlantic.com/technology/archive/2017/05/shadow-brokers/527778.

Selby, Nick, and Heather Vescent. *The Cyber Attack Survival Manual: Tools for Surviving Everything from Identity Theft to the Digital Apocalypse.* San Francisco, CA: Weldon Owen, 2017.

Shane, Scott, Nicole Periroth, and David E. Sanger. "Security Breach and Spilled Secrets Have Shaken the N.S.A. to Its Core." *New York Times*, November 12, 2017. https://www.nytimes.com/2017/11/12/us/nsa-shadow-brokers.html.

Index

About the Author

Kristi Lew has written numerous books for young people. Fascinated with science from a young age, she studied biochemistry and genetics in college. As a full-time science and technology writer, she spends an amazing amount of time poking around the internet. When she's not writing about or researching what's new in the world of science and crime, she can often be found trying to pry her latest mystery novel out from under the furry body of one of her three feline officemates.

Photo Credits

Cover Bill Hinton/Moment/Getty Images; pp. 4–5 Gorodenkoff/Shutterstock.com; p. 8 Pe3k/Shutterstock.com; p. 10 Matthew Lloyd/Getty Images; p. 12 Jonathan Storey AFP/Newscom; p. 15 Caiaimage/Paul Bradbury/Getty Images; p. 17 PeopleImages/E+/Getty Images; p. 20 Odd Andersen/AFP/Getty Images; p. 22 vectorsector/Shutterstock.com; p. 24 Nicescene/Shutterstock.com; p. 27 Tero Vesalainen/Shutterstock.com; pp. 29, 32, 48–49 © AP Images; p. 35 Donat Sorokin/TASS/Getty Images; p. 38 Drew Angerer/Getty Images; pp. 40–41 NurPhoto/Getty Images; p. 42 AFP Contributor/Getty Images; p. 45 designer491/Shutterstock.com; p. 50 Jack Guez/AFP/Getty Images; cover and interior pages background image (circuit board) jijomathai/Shutterstock.com; additional interior pages circuit board image gandroni/Shutterstock.com.

Design and Layout: Brian Garvey; Senior Editor: Kathy Kuhtz Campbell; Photo Researcher: Sherri Jackson